Bible-based activities to strengthen Christian values

The buyer of this book may reproduce pages for classroom or home use. Duplication for any other use is prohibited without written permission from David C. Cook Publishing Co.

Copyright ©1995 David C. Cook Publishing Co. Printed in the United States of America.

All puzzles and Bible activities are based on the NIV.

Scripture taken from the Holy Bible, New International Version, Copyright ©1973, 1978, 1984, International Bible Society. Used by permission of Zondervan Bible Publishers.

ISBN: 0-7814-5108-6

Edited by Debbie Bible
Book Design by Jack Rogers
Cover Illustration by Corbin Hillam
Interior Illustrations by Dana Regan & Corbin Hillam

TABLE OF CONTENTS

Introduction for Adult Friends of Children 3-4
What Is Being Unselfish? 5
The Bible Tells about Being Unselfish
   God Gives His Son, Jesus 6-7
Jesus Is Unselfish 8
Bible Words about Being Unselfish 9
Being Unselfish with Your Time 10
Practice Being Unselfish 11
Look for Ways to Help Others 12
A Wonder Ball to Share 13
The Bible Tells about Being Unselfish
   A Boy Shares His Lunch 14-15
Puppets for a Play about Being Unselfish 16-17
Sharing with Jesus
   A Puppet Play Based on John 6:1-15 18-19
Unselfish and a Part of a Miracle 20
Looking for Ways to Be Unselfish 21
Is This Being Unselfish? 22
The Value of Being Unselfish 23

What Is Being Prayerful? 24
The Bible Tells about Being Prayerful
   Jesus Teaches the Disciples to Pray 25-26
Jesus' Prayer Is an Example for Us 27
The Lord's Prayer 28
Praying with Thanks 29
What Do You Think about Prayer? 30
I Can Pray Any Time 31
Cheer-Up Prayer Cube 32
Write a Prayer 33
God Wants You to Pray Every Day 34
Prayer Is Powerful 35
The Bible Tells about Being Prayerful
   Daniel Prays Three Times Every Day 36-37
Lions and Daniel's Praying 38
Being Prayerful Is Doing What Is Right 39
What to Pray About 40
Make a Bag of Colors 41
The Value of Being Prayerful 42
Value Builders Series Index 43-48

UNSELFISH & PRAYERFUL

INTRODUCTION FOR ADULT FRIENDS OF CHILDREN
(Parents, Teachers, and Other Friends of Children)

Values. What are they? How do we acquire them? Can we change them?

"Values" is a popular term, usually meaning *the standard that governs how one acts and conducts one's life.* Our personal standards, or values, are learned and adapted, possibly changed and relearned, over a lifetime of experiences and influences. Children begin acquiring personal values at birth. As parents, teachers, and other adults who love children, we are concerned that they are learning worthwhile values, rather than being randomly influenced by everything around them. By God's design, we cannot control the process of acquiring values, but we can influence the process in a variety of ways. Our consistent modeling of biblical values is a vital influence, but children must also be encouraged to talk about specific values and be aware of these values in action in themselves and others.

These biblical values are God's values. He has established His standards to help us know how to live our lives and how we are to treat other people. Our goal is to have these biblical values be a part of each child's experience.

A value becomes one's own when a person chooses to act on that value consistently. Saying that we hold to the value of honesty, yet bending the truth or telling a lie when pressured, is a contradiction.

Providing opportunities for children to investigate a specific value, identifying with people in the Bible who have that value, and trying to put it into practice in real life situations will help strengthen the value in the lives of the children and reinforce its importance. The purpose of the Value Builders Series is to provide such opportunities.

This book in the Value Builders Series focuses on **being unselfish** and **being prayerful**. Being unselfish is *showing concern about the feelings and needs of others instead of thinking only about yourself.* The basis of our Christian faith is an example of unselfishness. Jesus showed His concern for us instead of for Himself by accepting the agony and pain of death on a cross. Another biblical example of unselfishness is the boy who gave his lunch to Jesus. Jesus miraculously increased that lunch, and it fed over five thousand people.

Being prayerful is *always being aware of God's presence, listening to God, and talking to God.* The disciples asked Jesus to teach them to pray. We follow their example. Daniel was very faithful in his daily prayer of thanksgiving to God.

3

UNSELFISH & PRAYERFUL

When other officials managed to get Daniel in trouble for his praying, God was honored throughout the land for His power and protection.

The Value Builders Series provides Bible story activities, craft activities, and life application activities that focus on specific biblical values. These books can be used by children working alone, or the pages can be reproduced and used in a classroom setting.

In a classroom setting, this book could be used to supplement curriculum that you are using, or it can be used as a curriculum itself in a 30-55 minute period. Each page is coded at the bottom to suggest where it might fit in a teaching session. The codes are as follows:

 = Definition page

 = Bible Story page

= Craft page

= Life Application page

Some suggestions for using the materials in this book in a 30-55 minute period are:

5-10 minutes:	Introduce the value and discuss the definition. Use pages entitled, "What Is Being Unselfish?" or "What Is Being Prayerful?"
10-15 minutes:	Present one of the Bible stories, using appropriate pages. Encourage the children to describe what it might have been like to be in that situation and what other things could have happened.
10-20 minutes:	Choose life application activity pages or craft activities that are appropriate to the children in your class. Design some group applications for the pages you have chosen.
5-10 minutes:	To conclude, use the page entitled, "The Value of Being Unselfish," or "The Value of Being Prayerful" and encourage the children to make a commitment to focus on this value for the next few days or weeks. Pray for God's help to guide the children as they learn to live by His standards.

WHAT IS BEING UNSELFISH?

BEING UNSELFISH IS...**showing concern about the feelings and needs of others instead of thinking only about yourself.**

I think being unselfish can also mean _____
_____

✎ **Circle the one who is being unselfish.**

Being unselfish is important to me.
When I spend time thinking about the feelings and needs of others instead of only thinking about myself, then being unselfish becomes one of my values.

Name _____

Date _____

God's values are the STANDARD to help me know how to live my life and treat other people

THE BIBLE TELLS ABOUT BEING UNSELFISH

God Gives His Son, Jesus

John 3:16; Luke 23:1-4; 23:21—24:6

For God so loved the world that he gave his one and only Son, that whoever believes in him shall not perish but have eternal life.

"ETERNAL LIFE" MEANS TO LIVE FOREVER IN HEAVEN WITH JESUS.

Then the whole assembly rose and led [Jesus] off to Pilate. And they began to accuse him . . .

Then Pilate announced to the chief priests and the crowd, "I find no basis for a charge against this man. . . ."

But they kept shouting, "Crucify him! Crucify him!"

For the third time he spoke to them: "Why? What crime has this man committed? I have found in him no grounds for the death penalty. Therefore I will have him punished and then release him."

But with loud shouts they insistently demanded that he be crucified, and their shouts prevailed. So Pilate decided to grant their demand. . . and surrendered Jesus to their will.

As they led him away, they seized Simon from Cyrene, who was on his way in from the country, and put the cross on him and made him carry it behind Jesus. A large number of people followed him . . . .

Two other men, both criminals, were also led out with him to be executed. When they came to the place called the Skull, there they crucified him, along with the criminals—one on his right, the other on his left. Jesus said, "Father, forgive them, for they do not know what they are doing.". . .

The people stood watching . . . The soldiers also came up and mocked him. . . .

(Read the rest of this story on page 7)

✎ **Use the letters in the word O T H E R S to fill in the missing letters.**

Jesus was un ___ ___ lfi ___ ___ because

He was more c ___ nc ___ ___ n ___ d about others than about Him ___ ___ lf.

The gua ___ d ___ and people hu ___ ___ and made fun of Je ___ u ___ , even though he had done n ___ ___ ___ ing w ___ ___ ng.

6

THE BIBLE TELLS ABOUT BEING UNSELFISH

God Gives His Son, Jesus

(John 3:16; Luke 23:1-4; 23:21—24:6 continued from page 6)

There was a written notice above him, which read: THIS IS THE KING OF THE JEWS.

One of the criminals who hung there hurled insults at him: "Aren't you the Christ? Save yourself and us!"

But the other criminal rebuked him. "Don't you fear God," he said, "since you are under the same sentence? We are punished justly, for we are getting what our deeds deserve. But this man has done nothing wrong."

Then he said, "Jesus, remember me when you come into your kingdom."

Jesus answered him, "I tell you the truth, today you will be with me in paradise."

It was now about the sixth hour, and darkness came over the whole land until the ninth hour, for the sun stopped shining. And the curtain of the temple was torn in two. Jesus called out with a loud voice, "Father, into your hands I commit my spirit." When he had said this, he breathed his last.

The centurion, seeing what had happened, praised God and said, "Surely this was a righteous man." . . .

On the first day of the week, very early in the morning, the women . . . entered [Jesus' tomb, but] they did not find the body of the Lord Jesus. While they were wondering about this, suddenly two men in clothes that gleamed like lightning stood beside them . . . [and] said to them, "Why do you look for the living among the dead? He is not here; he has risen!"

✎ Draw a line to show who said each.

"I can't find a reason to have Jesus killed."	Jesus
"Crucify him!"	Pilate
"Father, forgive them."	crowd of people
"We broke the law. But this man hasn't done anything wrong."	Jesus
"Today you will be with me in paradise."	centurion
"Father, I give you my spirit."	one of the criminals
"This was a righteous man."	Jesus

JESUS IS UNSELFISH

✏ **Circle the words from the word box that you see in the Bible story on pages 6 and 7. Then, see if you can do this crossword.**

WORD BOX

assembly
accuse
crucify
prevailed
criminals
executed
rebuked
sentence
commit
risen

ACROSS
1. crowd of people
2. kill by hanging on a cross
3. succeeded in convincing him
7. persons who have broken the law
8. punishment for breaking the law
9. scolded or corrected

DOWN
1. say he had done something wrong
4. killed
5. give to you
6. came back to life again

WORDS, WORDS, EVERYWHERE! TOO MANY WORDS TO LEARN.

KEEP THINKING. EVEN YOU CAN'T LEARN EVERYTHING IN ONE DAY.

✏ **Write here any other words from the Bible story you don't understand. Ask a trusted adult to help you learn what they mean.**

8

BIBLE WORDS ABOUT BEING UNSELFISH

Use the words in each box to finish the Bible verse, Romans 15:1-3.

bear   ourselves   the   failings   please   weak   of   the   with

We who are strong ought to b_____ w_____ t_____
f_____ o_____ t_____ w_____ and
not to p_____ o_____.

Can you think of someone who is weak in an area that you are strong?
What could you do to help that person?

Do you "build up" a person like a building?   No, you are nice and helpful to a person.

To "bear" means to be patient and concerned.

build   him   neighbor   to   good   his   please   up

Each of us should p_____ h_____ n_____
for his g_____, t_____ b_____ h_____ u___.

What is something you can do to please a friend?

for   please   even   himself   Christ   not   did

F____ e_____ C_____ d_____ n_____ p_____
h_____ . . .

How did Jesus show His unselfishness to us?

BEING UNSELFISH WITH YOUR TIME

Troy's Sunday school class has worked together to make cookies to share with the people living at the Seniors Lodge near the church. It's now Saturday afternoon and everyone is coming for the cookie party.

✏️ **Help them find the way from their homes to the Seniors Lodge by drawing along the path each could follow.**

Let's hop in Troy's pocket so we can join the cookie party.

I'll bring some chocolate-covered flies.

10

PRACTICE BEING UNSELFISH

When you are on a sports team, you know all about practice. You practice to learn the skills of the game, and you practice to work together as a team. When you want to improve, what do you do? Practice!

Now's the time to practice being unselfish. Here are some things to get you started.

Do you know three unselfish people?
✎ **Write their names.**

1. _____
2. _____
3. _____

Look for a time to talk to each of these "coaches" about how they can help you practice being unselfish.

✎ **Write three ways to be unselfish. Then, circle the one that you will practice this week.**

1. _____
2. _____
3. _____

IS IT UNSELFISH IF I TEACH YOU MY SECRET SHORT JUMP?

THAT'S THE SECRET!

BUT YOU ONLY DO THE LONG JUMP.

During the week, ask God to help you notice when you are being selfish, and to help you practice being unselfish instead.

LOOK FOR WAYS TO HELP OTHERS

✏️ **Finish each math sentence and then match the number answer to one of the lines below. Write the matching words on the lines and then read the Bible verse, Philippians 2:4.**

3 + 1 = _____ = also
1 + 2 = _____ = each
3 - 3 = _____ = look
3 + 4 = _____ = of
6 + 6 = _____ = others

5 - 3 = _____ = but
8 - 7 = _____ = interests
4 + 1 = _____ = not
10 - 1 = _____ = only
7 - 1 = _____ = own

7 + 7 = _____ = your
5 + 5 = _____ = to
10 - 2 = _____ = you
10 + 5 = _____ = should
15 - 4 = _____ = the

" _____ _____ _____ _____ _____
   3   7   8   15   0

_____ _____ _____ _____ _____
  5   9   10   14   6

_____ , _____ _____ _____ _____
  1   2   4   10   11

_____ _____ _____ ." Philippians 2:4
  1   7   12

"INTERESTS" ARE THE THINGS YOU NEED, SUCH AS FOOD, CLOTHES, A HOME, AND ALSO THE THINGS YOU LIKE OR WANT TO DO.

What are some of your interests?
_____

What are some interests of someone you know?
_____

How can you help take care of the interests of that other person?
_____

A WONDER BALL TO SHARE

A Wonder Ball is a great way to share small gifts and surprises with your friends at a party or other event. A Wonder Ball is a "round" object made of crepe paper and filled with lots of small items, such as candy and toys.

You need:
- ☐ 1 roll of crepe paper (2-3 inches wide) or 2 packages of crepe paper cut into 2-3 inch strips
- ☐ Tape
- ☐ Small items such as wrapped candy, games, erasers, toys, or a folded paper with a written puzzle, a fun note, or a Bible verse (enough for each person to have the same amount)

✂ To make a Wonder Ball:
1. Hold the largest item and wrap a strip of crepe paper around it in different directions until the object is completely covered.
2. Place another item against the wrapped object and continue winding the crepe paper around it to hold it in place and completely hide it.
3. Continue adding items, one at a time, completely covering each item before adding the next one and using more strips of crepe paper as needed.
4. When all the items are hidden in the ball, finish winding the last strip of crepe paper and tape it to the ball to keep it from unwinding.

✂ To use the Wonder Ball:
1. Each participant unwinds the ball just far enough to find an item, which that person keeps, and then passes the ball on to the next person.
2. The unwinding and finding continues around the circle until all the items have been discovered.

THE BIBLE TELLS ABOUT BEING UNSELFISH

A Boy Shares His Lunch

John 6:1-15

Jesus crossed to the far shore of the Sea of Galilee (that is, the Sea of Tiberias), and a great crowd of people followed him because they saw the miraculous signs he had performed on the sick. Then Jesus went up on a mountainside and sat down with his disciples. The Jewish Passover Feast was near.

When Jesus looked up and saw a great crowd coming toward him, he said to Philip, "Where shall we buy bread for these people to eat?" He asked this only to test him, for he already had in mind what he was going to do.

Philip answered him, "Eight months' wages would not buy enough bread for each one to have a bite!"

Another of his disciples, Andrew, Simon Peter's brother, spoke up, "Here is a boy with five small barley loaves and two small fish, but how far will they go among so many?"

(Read the rest of this story on page 15)

✏ Put a check by the answer to each question.

What did Jesus say when he saw all the people?
　　___ "Where can we buy food for all these people?"
　　___ "Shall we go fishing together next week?"

What did Philip tell Jesus?
　　___ "It would cost too much money to buy enough food."
　　___ "Tell the people to go home and eat there."

What did the boy have in his lunch?
　　___ Two apples and some juice
　　___ Two dried fish and five small loaves of bread

Who told Jesus about the boy's food?
　　___ One of the crowd
　　___ Andrew

THE BIBLE TELLS ABOUT BEING UNSELFISH

A Boy Shares His Lunch

(John 6:1-15 continued from page 14)

Jesus said, "Have the people sit down." There was plenty of grass in that place, and the men sat down, about five thousand of them. Jesus then took the loaves, gave thanks, and distributed to those who were seated as much as they wanted. He did the same with the fish.

When they had all had enough to eat, he said to his disciples, "Gather the pieces that are left over. Let nothing be wasted." So they gathered them and filled twelve baskets with the pieces of the five barley loaves left over by those who had eaten.

"PROPHET" MEANS ONE WHO TELLS PEOPLE ABOUT GOD.

After the people saw the miraculous sign that Jesus did, they began to say, "Surely this is the Prophet who is to come into the world." Jesus, knowing that they intended to come and make him king by force, withdrew again to a mountain by himself.

✏️ **Draw lines to connect these sentences that tell about the story. The first one has been done for you.**

1. The crowd	about the boy's	food to the people.
2. The boy told	God and gave the	to see the miracles.
3. Andrew told Jesus	followed Jesus	about his lunch.
4. Jesus thanked	food for	bread and fish.
5. There was enough	Jesus	was a prophet.
6. The people said	Andrew	all the people.

15

PUPPETS FOR A PLAY ABOUT BEING UNSELFISH

Make puppets and background pieces to use with the puppet play on pages 18 and 19.

✂ **To make puppets and props:**
1. Cut out puppets and decorate.
2. Cut out leg holes where your fingers will go.
3. Attach chenille wires where indicated to make arms.
4. Make 12 baskets using the patterns on page 17.

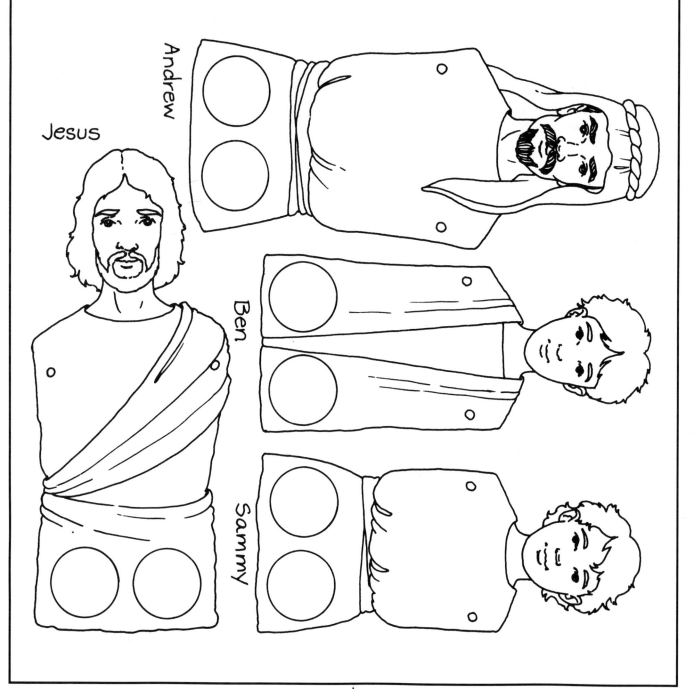

PUPPETS FOR A PLAY ABOUT BEING UNSELFISH

SHARING WITH JESUS

A Puppet Play Based on John 6:1-15

The people in this story are: Ben (the boy with a lunch), Sammy (Ben's friend), Jesus, Andrew, Philip, group of disciples, and a large crowd.

PREPARATION:
1. Follow the directions for making the puppets and background pieces on pages 16 and 17.
2. You may want to make some paper trees and grass background for this outdoor scene.

SETTING: This takes place in the countryside near the Sea of Galilee, on a small mountainside.

[The crowd of STANDING PEOPLE are at the back. JESUS, ANDREW, PHILIP, and the other DISCIPLES are sitting by the crowd near the left side. BEN (carrying lunch basket) and SAMMY enter center. BEN stoops and pretends to pick up something and tosses it to Sammy, who pretends to throw it back.]

SAMMY: I'll race you to that tree. Toss your lunch down and let's go! *(starts running then looks back at BEN, who had started running and then stops suddenly)*

BEN: Look! Over there! Why are all these people out here in the country? There must be hundreds of them!

SAMMY *(stops and looks)*: More than hundreds, Ben. Probably thousands; they go on forever. Let's go see what's happening!

[BEN and SAMMY run back and get BEN'S lunch and then run toward the edge of the crowd, stage right. They move through the crowd, but are hidden as they move behind the crowd and enter again stage left, just at the edge of the crowd.]

BEN *(whispering as they walk along in front of the crowd)*: Look! It's Jesus! I know about Him! Some say He is the Son of God come to earth!

SAMMY: Shh! I can hear the men talking. Listen.

[BEN and SAMMY move closer to JESUS and the DISCIPLES.]

JESUS *(to PHILIP)*: Where can we buy bread for these people to eat?

PHILIP: Buy bread? How much money would that take? Even if you worked for months, you couldn't earn enough money to buy all the bread to give each person just one bite! There is no way we can feed these people!

BEN *(whispering to SAMMY)*: Did you hear that? I'm going to give my lunch to Jesus. Maybe he can use it.

SAMMY: Hey, if you don't want it, give it to me.

[BEN moves closer to the men. ANDREW turns and sees them.]

ANDREW: Hi! I'm Andrew.

18

SHARING WITH JESUS

BEN: Hi, I'm Ben and this is Sammy. We couldn't help overhearing that you need some food. Here's my lunch. Would you give it to Jesus for me? I'd like him to have it. *(holds out basket)*

ANDREW: That's very unselfish of you. I'll take it to Jesus. *(takes the basket from BEN and turns to JESUS)* Master, here is a boy with a lunch basket. He wants to give it to you. *(looks in the basket)* It's five small loaves of barley bread and two small dried fish. He's certainly unselfish, but it won't feed this crowd!

JESUS: Please ask the people to sit down.

[Change the background crowd of standing people to the one of sitting people as PETER, ANDREW, and the other DISCIPLES walk around asking the people to tell other people that everyone should be seated in groups on the grass.]

JESUS *(praying)*: Thank you, Father, for this food. *(to the disciples)* Please give some of these fish and bread to the people around you and ask them to share with those near them. Maybe Ben and Sammy would like to help you.

[BEN, SAMMY, ANDREW, PHILIP and the DISCIPLES take the food from JESUS as he breaks it apart and gives it to some people nearby. JESUS continues to break apart the bread and fish, and they keep giving it out, asking the people to pass it on.]

BEN *(quietly to himself, looking around at all the people who are now eating)*: But, why isn't the food all gone? How can there be so much? Jesus keeps breaking off pieces of the bread and fish and there is always more.

JESUS *(to ANDREW and PHILIP)*: When all the people have eaten, gather the pieces that are left over. Don't let anything be wasted.

[BEN and SAMMY help the disciples gather all the food. Some of the people have baskets that they put it in. Twelve are filled with leftovers.]

BEN *(to SAMMY)*: Listen to the people in the crowd! They know this is a miracle! The food just keeps coming and coming! What are the people saying?

SAMMY: It sounds like they are saying that Jesus is a prophet who has come here from God. Wow!

ANDREW *(to BEN)*: Thank you for sharing your lunch with Jesus. Now ALL the people have had enough to eat.

BEN *(looking toward where JESUS is standing)*: Just think! JESUS used MY lunch to perform a miracle like that! I'm glad I gave it to him.

[BEN, SAMMY and ANDREW turn toward JESUS as JESUS calls to the disciples.]

JESUS: I'm going further up on this mountain to rest and be alone for awhile. I'll see you again soon.

[JESUS exits stage left and the others watch him go and then everyone exits.]

UNSELFISH AND A PART OF A MIRACLE

Read the Bible story on pages 14 and 15 or in your Bible in John 6.

Pretend that you were the boy who gave his food to Jesus. **Write a letter to or draw a picture for your friend telling or showing how you felt about what happened.**

What do you think was the most exciting part of the story about the boy who gave his food to Jesus? _____

_____

20

LOOKING FOR WAYS TO BE UNSELFISH

Your eyes and ears can help you know when someone needs or wants something.

✎ **Use the code to find out what unselfish thought this person is thinking. Then finish drawing the face so it looks like you.**

1 = A   2 = C   3 = D
4 = E   5 = H   6 = I
7 = L   8 = N   9 = O
10 = P 11 = T 12 = U
13 = W 14 = Y

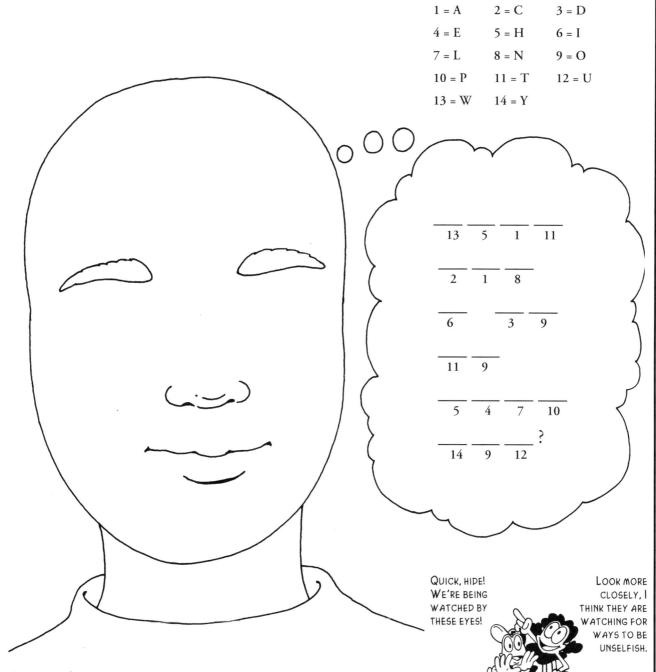

__ __ __ __
13 5 1 11

__ __ __
2 1 8

__ __ __
6 3 9

__ __
11 9

__ __ __ __
5 4 7 10

__ __ __ ?
14 9 12

QUICK, HIDE! WE'RE BEING WATCHED BY THESE EYES!

LOOK MORE CLOSELY, I THINK THEY ARE WATCHING FOR WAYS TO BE UNSELFISH.

Remember:
Eyes can look and ears can listen for ways to be unselfish.

IS THIS BEING UNSELFISH?

Do you say things to show you are thinking about what someone else might want and need? Or are you thinking only about yourself? ✏ **Read what these kids are saying and circle the right word.**

UNSELFISH is thinking about others and what they want and need.

SELFISH is thinking <u>only</u> about yourself and what you want and need.

"Give me all the ice cream." UNSELFISH SELFISH

"Can I help you?" UNSELFISH SELFISH

"What will I get if I help you?" UNSELFISH SELFISH

"You can't have this ball now, but I'll let you have it next." UNSELFISH SELFISH

"I'll help you if you give me something." UNSELFISH SELFISH

"We can share this cookie." UNSELFISH SELFISH

"I don't want to help you." UNSELFISH SELFISH

When you want to say "What will you give me if I do it?"

and do this instead

1. Ask God to help you be unselfish.

2. Think about the other person and not just yourself.

3. Look for things to do without always expecting a reward.

THE VALUE OF BEING UNSELFISH

God's values are the STANDARD to help me know how to live my life and treat other people

HOW CAN YOU KNOW WHAT YOUR VALUES ARE? Look at the things you DO, SAY, and THINK. If you spend time doing something, then you know it is one of your values.

Are you thinking what is in the thought balloon?

My name is _____ .

Being unselfish _____ important to me.
                 is   is not

I _____ spend time showing concern for the feelings and needs of others
  do   do not
instead of thinking only about myself.

Thinking about what someone else needs or wants instead of thinking only about myself is being unselfish.

I can show that being unselfish is becoming my value when

I _____ and _____

✏ **Write a television commercial for a new product that can help people learn to be unselfish.**

23

WHAT IS BEING PRAYERFUL?

BEING PRAYERFUL IS . . . **always being aware of God's presence, listening to God, and talking to Him.**

I think being prayerful can also mean _____
_____

Some of the letters are missing in this important fact. **Use the letters in the underlined sentence to finish the words:**

<u>God is right here.</u>   (d,e,g,h,i,o,r,s,t)

G __ __   __ __   w __ __ __

m __   all   __ __ __   t __ m __

an __   I can l __ __ __ __ n

an __   __ a l k   __ o   H __ m

any   __ __ m __ !

Being prayerful is important to me.
When I am aware that God is always with me and I listen and talk to Him, then being prayerful becomes one of my values.

Name _____

Date _____

God's values are the STANDARD to help me know how to live my life and treat other people

THE BIBLE TELLS ABOUT BEING PRAYERFUL

Jesus Teaches the Disciples to Pray

Luke 11:1-4

One day Jesus was praying in a certain place. When he finished, one of his disciples said to him, "Lord, teach us to pray, just as John taught his disciples."

He said to them, "When you pray, say:
"'Father, hallowed be your name,
your kingdom come.
Give us each day our daily bread.
Forgive us our sins,
for we also forgive everyone who sins against us.
And lead us not into temptation.'"

✏️ **Draw a picture of the disciples sitting with Jesus, talking about praying.**

DOES GOD ONLY GIVE PEOPLE BREAD TO EAT? WHAT ABOUT PIZZA, ICE CREAM, GRAPES, AND CRAB SALAD? "BREAD" MEANS ALL FOOD AND OTHER THINGS THEY NEED TO LIVE.

✏️ **Draw a line to show another way to say about the same thing as these words from Jesus' prayer.**

1. Father   we give honor to your name

2. hallowed be your name   God

3. daily bread   keep us away from doing wrong

4. lead not to temptation   the food and things we need every day

25

THE BIBLE TELLS ABOUT BEING PRAYERFUL

Jesus Teaches the Disciples to Pray

Here are other verses in the Bible about Jesus teaching his disciples how to pray.

Matthew 6:5-15

"And when you pray, do not be like the hypocrites, for they love to pray standing in the synagogues and on the street corners to be seen by men. I tell you the truth, they have received their reward in full. But when you pray, go into your room, close the door and pray to your Father, who is unseen. Then your Father, who sees what is done in secret, will reward you. And when you pray, do not keep on babbling like pagans, for they think they will be heard because of their many words. Do not be like them, for your Father knows what you need before you ask him. 'This, then, is how you should pray:

"'Our Father in heaven, hallowed be your name, your kingdom come,
your will be done on earth as it is in heaven.
Give us today our daily bread.
Forgive us our debts, as we also have forgiven our debtors.
And lead us not into temptation, but deliver us from the evil one.'

For if you forgive men when they sin against you, your heavenly Father will also forgive you. But if you do not forgive men their sins, your Father will not forgive your sins."

✎ **Put a check by the things Jesus told the disciples about praying. Put an X by the things Jesus did not say.**

Jesus said:

___ "Be honest and sincere when you pray, not like hypocrites who say one thing and mean another."

___ "God doesn't want people to pray; He is too busy."

___ "Pray because you want to talk to God, not because you want other people to see what you are doing."

___ "Use words to tell God what you want to say, but don't just say the same words over and over again."

JESUS' PRAYER IS AN EXAMPLE FOR US

The prayer that Jesus taught his disciples shows us things we should include in our prayers. **What are the four things we are to do when we pray the way Jesus taught us to pray? Write these words where you see this picture code to find out.**

◯ = God   👄 = Ask   ✋ = Give   👫 = us   🙍 = forgive   📖 = right

1. _____ honor to _____'s name.
   ✋   ◯

2. _____ _____ to _____ _____ what we
   👄   ◯   ✋   👫
   need each day.

   "HALLOWED" AND "HONOR" MEAN TO RESPECT.

3. _____ _____ to _____ _____ for what
   👄   ◯   🙍   👫
   we have done wrong and help _____ to _____ others.
                                 👫   🙍

4. _____ _____ for help to do what is _____ and to
   👄   ◯   📖
   lead us away from doing wrong things.

27

THE LORD'S PRAYER

The prayer that Jesus taught His disciples is often used as a prayer that we all pray together in church or on special occasions. **Cut these word strips apart, mix them up, and then arrange them in order. Set two or three aside and arrange the other strips, saying the words for the missing strips. Do this several times until you can say the Lord's Prayer from memory without looking at any of the word strips.**

WATCH OUT FOR SCISSORS ON THIS PAGE!

YOU'RE A GREAT CUT-UP ANYWAY. I LIKE YOU TO MAKE ME LAUGH!

If you want to know the word order after you have cut the word strips apart, look in your Bible, Matthew 6 (KJV).

Our Father which art in Heaven,
Hallowed be thy name.
Thy kingdom come.
Thy will be done in earth, as it is in heaven.
Give us this day our daily bread.
And forgive us our debts, as we forgive our debtors.
And lead us not into temptation,
but deliver us from evil:
For thine is the kingdom,
and the power, and the glory, for ever. Amen.

PRAYING WITH THANKS

Telling God you are thankful is an important part of being prayerful. ✎ **Color each section as marked and discover this picture about telling God "thank you."**   1 = red   2 = yellow   3 = green   4 = blue   5 = brown

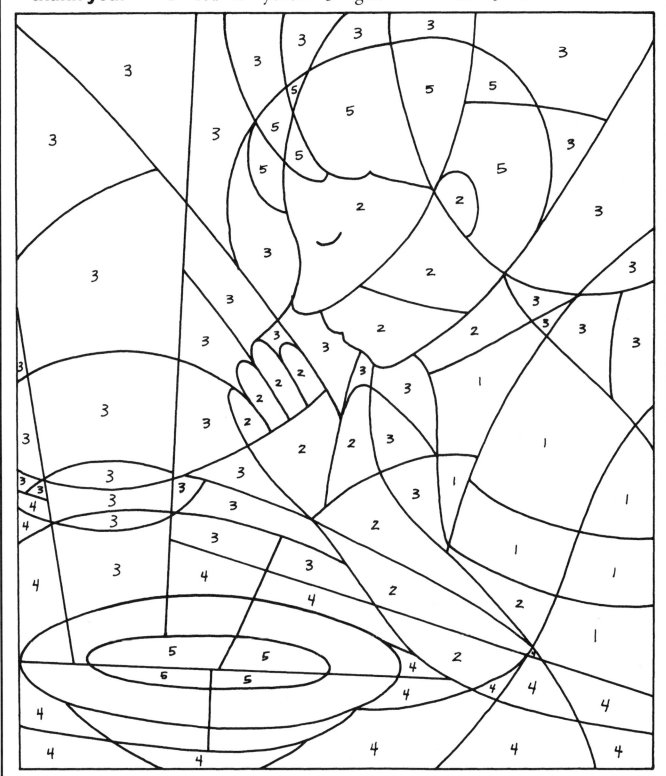

WHAT DO YOU THINK ABOUT PRAYER?

When someone asks you a question about prayer, what do you say? ✎ **See what these friends are asking and then put a mark by what you would answer or write your own answers on the lines.**

1.____ I don't think it matters whether we pray or not. I know lots of kids who don't pray and I don't think they are any different than we are.

2.____ God created us and planned that we could talk and listen to Him as one way to show our love for Him. God thought of prayer as a good way for people to be a part of His plan for the world.

3._____

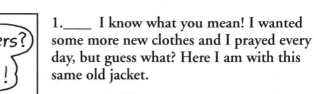

1.____ I know what you mean! I wanted some more new clothes and I prayed every day, but guess what? Here I am with this same old jacket.

2.____ God loves you very much and wants what is best for you. That's why He answers some prayers "yes," some prayers "no," and some prayers "wait."

3._____

1.____ God is Spirit and He IS with you all the time. Ask Him to help you know that He is there even when it doesn't feel like He is near.

2.____ You're right. God can only be in one place at a time, so He probably isn't with you when you pray.

3._____

I CAN PRAY ANY TIME

✎ Write the first letter of each picture on the line above it. Write your name each time you see an empty box.

GOD is __ __ __ __ __ __ with [   ]

so [   ] can TALK to GOD and

GOD can TALK to [   ]

anytime and anywhere! GOD talks to [   ] in

__ __ __ __ __ __ when [   ]

__ __ __ __ __ __ __ __ to hear GOD.

CHEER-UP PRAYER CUBE

When you want to let a friend know that you are praying for them, why not send them a Cheer-Up Prayer Cube?

You need:
- ☐ A square box
- ☐ Paint and paint brush
- ☐ Newspaper and glue
- ☐ Jokes, riddles, and funny pictures
- ☐ Yarn
- ☐ Markers

✂ **To make a Cheer-Up Prayer Cube:**

1. Cover your work area with newspaper.
2. Paint your box, then let it dry completely.
3. Decorate the box by gluing riddles, jokes, and funny pictures all around it. Be sure to leave a space for gluing a special message you may want to write to your friend.
4. Attach yarn for hanging.
5. Deliver the gift to your friend.

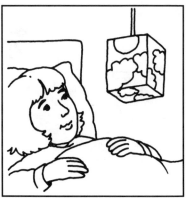

32

WRITE A PRAYER

What is a prayer? ✎ **Check the answers you think are correct.**
_____ writing a letter to God.
_____ writing down the words you say when you talk.
_____ writing a poem to God.

✎ **Choose one type of prayer and write it here.**
_____
_____
_____
_____
_____
_____
_____
_____

Here is a prayer written to God.

It is called the _____ _____ because Jesus
                              rod'sL   rayrep

taught this to His disciples.

> *Our Father which art in Heaven,*
> *Hallowed be thy name.*
> *Thy kingdom come.*
> *Thy will be done in earth, as it is in heaven.*
> *Give us this day our daily bread.*
> *And forgive us our debts, as we forgive our debtors.*
> *And lead us not into temptation,*
> *but deliver us from evil:*
> *For thine is the kingdom,*
> *and the power, and the glory, for ever. Amen.*

GOD WANTS YOU TO PRAY EVERY DAY

God is such a wonderful Friend. He wants you to visit with Him every day. Plan a time and a place so you will be sure to talk to God as often as you can.

WHEN: ✎ **Use these clocks to mark in a good time to talk to God each day. Draw the hands on the clocks to show the times.**

On school days   On weekends and vacations   On the Lord's Day

WHERE: ✎ **Draw a picture of a good place in your house or yard where you can be quiet and alone to visit with God every day.**

WHAT: ✎ **Read each statement below then color the ones that you do when you visit with God. The items that are underlined are always good to include. Write in one of your own ideas.**

- <u>Say thank you for something God did.</u>
- Write a prayer.
- Think about what you have read in the Bible.
- Thank God for taking care of the things you need.
- <u>Tell God about your day.</u>
- Tell God some of the wonderful things you know about Him.
- <u>Listen to God.</u>
- Tell God what you need.
- <u>Sing a song to God.</u>
- Read a short part in the Bible.
- Ask God to bless your time together.
- Tell God what your family, friends, and others need.

PRAYER IS POWERFUL

✎ Draw a line through these words to find the Bible verse, James 5:16. Follow these instructions, remembering to always move one box at a time in the direction indicated. Read the verse in your Bible when you are finished to see if you found all the words.

Start with (Confess), then move down a box to (your), move right to (sins), right, up, right, down, down, left, down, down, left, left, down, right, right, right, up, right, up, up, up, right, down, down, down, down.

START: ⬇

Confess	to	each	other	to	God
your	sins	to	and	righteous	man
prayer	with	for	pray	a	is
God	pray	each	God	of	powerful
that	so	other	The	prayer	and
you	may	be	healed.	is	effective.

✎ Start with A and cross out each letter that comes in the alphabet order. A, B, C, D, E, F, and so on. Write the letters that are left on the lines to find the meanings of the four words. One has been done for you.

1. A̶T̶B̶E̶C̶D̶L̶E̶T̶F̶H̶G̶E̶H̶T̶I̶R̶J̶U̶K̶T̶L̶H̶
2. MTNAOLPKQIRNSGTAUNVDWLXIYSZTAEBNCIDNEGFTGOHGIOJDK
3. DLOMINNOGPWQHRASTTIUSVRWIXGYHZT
4. ACBACNDHEEFLGPHTIOJCKHLAMNNGOEP

1. confess = T E L L ___ ___ ___ ___ ___ ___ ___ ___

2. prayer = ___ ___ ___ ___ ___ ___ ___ ___ ___ ___ ___ ___ ___ ___ ___ ___ ___ ___ ___ ___

___ ___ ___ ___ ___

3. righteous = ___ ___ ___ ___ ___ ___ ___ ___ ___ ___ ___ ___

4. effective = ___ ___ ___ ___ ___ ___ ___ ___ ___ ___ ___ ___ ___ ___ ___

One person I will pray for is _____ because _____

_____

35

THE BIBLE TELLS ABOUT BEING PRAYERFUL

Daniel Prays Three Times Every Day

Daniel 6:1-27

It pleased [King] Darius to appoint 120 satraps to rule throughout the kingdom, with three administrators over them, one of whom was Daniel. . . . Daniel so distinguished himself . . . by his exceptional qualities that the king planned to set him over the whole kingdom. At this, the administrators and the satraps tried to find grounds for charges against Daniel in his conduct of government affairs, but they were unable to do so. They could find no corruption in him, because he was trustworthy and neither corrupt nor negligent. Finally these men said, "We will never find any basis for charges against this man Daniel unless it has something to do with the law of his God."

"Distinguished" means he did important things that others noticed.

So [they] went as a group to the king and said: "O King Darius, . . . [we] have all agreed that [you] should issue an edict and enforce the decree that anyone who prays to any god or man during the next thirty days, except to you, O king, shall be thrown into the lions' den. . . ." So King Darius put the decree in writing.

Now when Daniel learned that the decree had been published, he went home to his upstairs room where the windows opened toward Jerusalem. Three times a day he got down on his knees and prayed, giving thanks to his God, just as he had done before. Then these men . . . found Daniel praying and asking God for help. . . .

"Distressed" means very concerned.

Then they said to the king, "Daniel . . . still prays three times a day." When the king heard this, he was greatly distressed; he was determined to rescue Daniel and made every effort until sundown to save him.

(Read the rest of this story on page 37)

✏ **The missing words are in a code that YOU have to figure out first. The code is either the letter in the alphabet that comes AFTER each letter or BEFORE each letter. (A comes after Z.)**

Three times every day _____ got down on his _____ and
       c-z-m-h-d-k   j-m-d-d-r

_____ , giving _____ to _____ .
   o-q-z-x-d-c   s-g-z-m-j-r   f-n-c

The other officials wanted _____ to stop _____ .
                              c-z-m-h-d-k   o-q-z-x-h-m-f

36

THE BIBLE TELLS ABOUT BEING PRAYERFUL

Daniel Prays Three Times Every Day

(Daniel 6:1-27 continued from page 36)

Then the men . . . said to [the king], "Remember, O king . . . no decree or edict that the king issues can be changed."

So the king gave the order, and they brought Daniel and threw him into the lions' den. The king said to Daniel, "May your God, whom you serve continually, rescue you!"

A stone was brought and placed over the mouth of the den . . . Then the king returned to his palace and spent the night without eating. . . . And he could not sleep.

At the first light of dawn, the king got up and hurried to the lions' den. . . . He called to Daniel in an anguished voice, "Daniel, servant of the living God, has your God, whom you serve continually, been able to rescue you from the lions?"

Daniel answered, "O king, live forever! My God sent his angel, and he shut the mouths of the lions. They have not hurt me, . . ."

The king was overjoyed and gave orders to lift Daniel out of the den. And when Daniel was lifted from the den, no wound was found on him, because he had trusted in his God. . . .

Then King Darius wrote to all the peoples . . .

"I issue a decree that in every part of my kingdom people must fear and reverence the God of Daniel.

"For he is the living God and he endures forever; his kingdom will not be destroyed . . . He has rescued Daniel from the power of the lions."

"ENDURES" MEANS KEEPS GOING ON NO MATTER WHAT.

✏️ **Look in the Bible story to see who said these words. Write the names on the lines.**

 Daniel    King Darius

"May your God rescue you!" _____

"My God shut the mouths of the lions." _____

"People must reverence the God of Daniel." _____

"The lions have not hurt me." _____

"The God of Daniel is the living God." _____

37

LIONS AND DANIEL'S PRAYING

✏ **Read the Bible story on pages 36 and 37 or in your Bible in Daniel 6:1-27. Draw the picture or write the name to show who these sentences tell about.**

Daniel   King Darius   Some of the officials   Lions

- I foolishly let some of the officials make a law about prayer.
- I couldn't eat or sleep because I thought the lions would eat Daniel.
- I found out that Daniel's God IS powerful. He protected Daniel from the lions, and now I want God honored in all the land.

- Even though we hadn't eaten for a long time, we weren't interested in Daniel.
- We kept our mouths closed all night.

- We don't want Daniel to be more important than we are, so we tricked the king and made a law to kill him.
- We told the king that Daniel was disobeying the law and praying to God.

- The king appointed me to help him lead his kingdom.
- I pray to God every day by my open window.
- I am very thankful to God and nothing will stop me from praying.
- The lions didn't hurt me. It was a miracle! Now King Darius is honoring God!

BEING PRAYERFUL IS DOING WHAT IS RIGHT

The other men didn't like Daniel and wanted to get him in trouble with the King. They did get him in trouble—with lions! Read about it on pages 36 and 37 or in your Bible in Daniel 6.

But Daniel decided to keep on praying every day, because he knew it was the right thing to do. Like Daniel, you may have things or people that will make praying a hard thing for you to do, too. Follow the directions below:

✎ **List some things or people who make it hard for you to pray.**

_____   _____

_____   _____

✎ **Now, read each situation below and decide what you could say to each person. Write your answers on the lines provided.**

Caitlyn is home sick today and the Sunday school teacher asked us to pray for her. But Caitlyn always says mean things to me, so I don't want to pray for her!

I know that going to prayer meeting with my family is important. But I would rather go to the mall with my friends tonight.

This test is really hard and I know praying could help me. But I'm afraid someone might know that's what I am doing. Then they'll make fun of me.

39

WHAT TO PRAY ABOUT

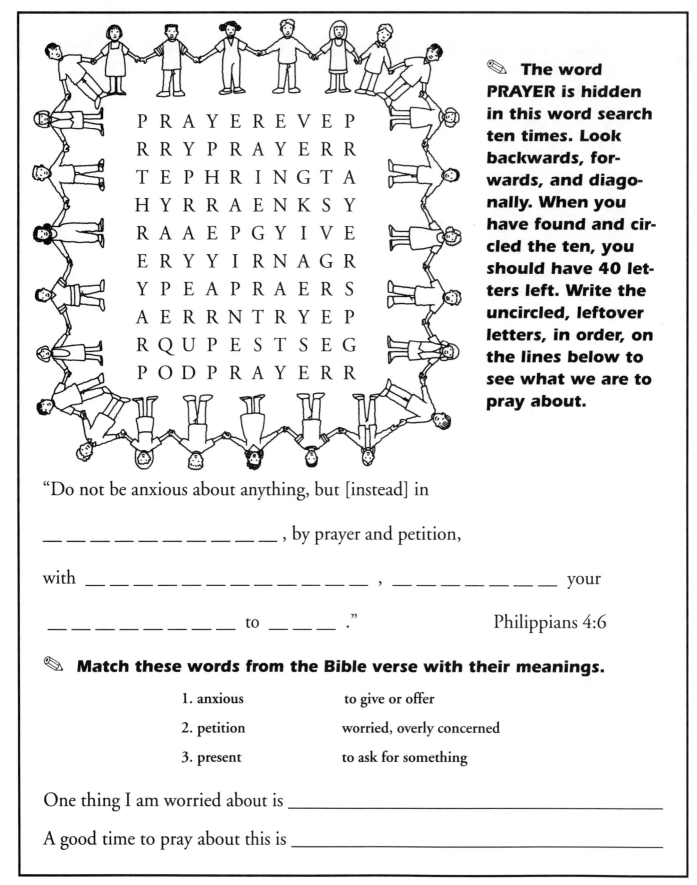

```
P R A Y E R E V E P
R R Y P R A Y E R R
T E P H R I N G T A
H Y R R A E N K S Y
R A A E P G Y I V E
E R Y Y I R N A G R
Y P E A P R A E R S
A E R R N T R Y E P
R Q U P E S T S E G
P O D P R A Y E R R
```

✎ **The word PRAYER is hidden in this word search ten times. Look backwards, forwards, and diagonally. When you have found and circled the ten, you should have 40 letters left. Write the uncircled, leftover letters, in order, on the lines below to see what we are to pray about.**

"Do not be anxious about anything, but [instead] in

_ _ _ _ _ _ _ _ _ _ _ , by prayer and petition,

with _ _ _ _ _ _ _ _ _ _ _ _ _ _ _ , _ _ _ _ _ _ _ your

_ _ _ _ _ _ _ _ _ to _ _ _ ."   Philippians 4:6

✎ **Match these words from the Bible verse with their meanings.**

    1. anxious   to give or offer

    2. petition   worried, overly concerned

    3. present   to ask for something

One thing I am worried about is _____

A good time to pray about this is _____

MAKE A BAG OF COLORS

There are many things to talk to God about. Make a Bag of Colors and keep some prayer ideas and reminders in it.

You need:
- ☐ 3 colors of poster paint, small amount of each in dishes
- ☐ 3-4-inch pieces of sponge
- ☐ 3-4 clip clothespins (to clip to sponge and use as a handle)
- ☐ A lunch-size paper bag
- ☐ Newspaper and glue
- ☐ 20 or more 3" x 5" cards
- ☐ Pictures of your family, friends, missionaries, and teachers
- ☐ Bible

To make a Bag of Colors:
1. Wrinkle several sheets of newspaper and put them inside the lunch bag so the bag can stand alone and all the sides are easy to paint.
2. Dip a sponge into the paint and blot or touch the paper bag in a few places.
3. Dip another sponge into a different color of paint and blot or touch the bag with that paint, putting some on all sides of the bag.
4. Continue this with the third color until the entire outside of the bag is covered with color.
5. Wait until the paint is dry and then remove the newspaper.

To make Prayer Reminders:
1. Glue pictures on 3" x 5" cards of the people you will be praying for.
2. Choose five Bible verses that you could use as a prayer, such as Psalm 119:105. Write out the words of each one on separate cards.
3. Think of five things you want to thank God for and write each of these on separate cards.
4. Put all these cards in your Bag of Colors.

To use your Bag of Colors
Each day, close your eyes, reach into your Bag of Colors and take out one or more cards. Pray for or about whatever is on the card.

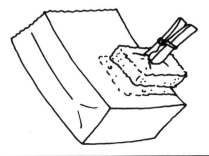
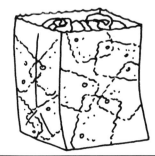

THE VALUE OF BEING PRAYERFUL

God's values are the STANDARD to help me know how to live my life and treat other people

How can you know what your values are? Look at the things you DO, SAY, and THINK. If you spend time doing something, then you know it is one of your values.

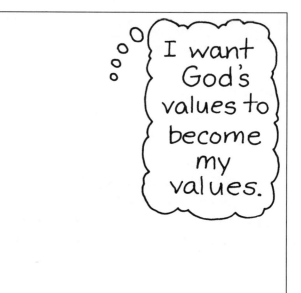

✏ **Draw a picture of yourself here.** Are you thinking what is in the thought balloon?

My name is _____.

Being prayerful _____ important to me.
                    is   is not

I _____ spend time talking and listening to God,
   do   do not
because He is always with me.

Knowing that God is with me all the time, and listening and talking to God is being prayerful.

I can show that being prayerful is becoming my value when I _____

_____ and _____.

✏ **Write a song to tell how you feel about God being right with you so you can talk and listen to Him anytime.**

VALUE BUILDERS SERIES INDEX
BY VALUE

Accepting
Romans 15:7
Galatians 3:28
Luke 7 — Jesus and the woman with no name
Acts 10 — Peter's vision and visit

Appreciative
See thankful

Attentive
Psalm 34:15
James 1:19
Nehemiah 8 — Ezra reads the law
Luke 10 — Mary listens to Jesus

Caring
See concerned

Choices
See wise

Committed
1 Kings 8:61
Proverbs 16:3
Esther 4 — Esther
John 1 — Andrew follows Jesus

Compassionate
2 Corinthians 1:3-4
1 Peter 3:8
Luke 10 — Good Samaritan
Luke 23 — Jesus on the cross

Concerned
1 Corinthians 12:25
1 John 3:17
Matthew 25 — Jesus teaches to meet needs
Acts 2 — Church provides for each other

Confident
Philippians 4:13
Psalm 139:14
1 Samuel 17 — David and Goliath
Nehemiah 6 — Nehemiah isn't intimidated

Considerate
See respectful, kind

Consistent
1 John 3:18
Psalm 33:4
Matthew 26 — Jesus in the garden
Daniel 6 — Daniel as administrator

Contented
See peaceful

Conviction
Deuteronomy 13:6-8
Acts 4:19-20
Daniel 3 — Blazing furnace and three Hebrews
John 2 — Jesus clears the temple courts

Cooperative
Colossians 3:23-24
Ephesians 4:16
Acts 6 — Disciples share responsibilities
Exodus 18 — Jethro gives Moses a plan

Courageous
Joshua 1:9
Isaiah 41:10
Acts 23 — Paul's nephew
Esther 4 — Esther

Creative
See resourceful

Decision Making
See purposeful

Dedicated
See committed

Dependable
See responsible

Diligent
See persevering, purposeful, responsible

Discerning
See wise

Discipleship
See teachable, prayerful, worshipful, faith, holy

Discipline
See self-disciplined

Empathy
Galatians 6:2
Hebrews 13:3
John 11 — Jesus at Lazarus's death
1 Samuel 19 — Jonathan speaks up for David

Endurance
See persevering, self-disciplined, purposeful

Enthusiasm
See joyful

Fairness
Leviticus 19:15
Romans 12:17
James 2 — Favoritism at a meeting
Matthew 20 — Parable of workers

Faith
John 3:16
Hebrews 11:6
Acts 16 — Philippian jailer
Matthew 8 — Centurion sends servant to Jesus

Faithful
See loyal

VALUE BUILDERS SERIES INDEX
BY VALUE

Fellowship
See friendly

Flexibility
See cooperative, initiative, resourceful

Forgiving
Ephesians 4:32
Leviticus 19:18
Matthew 18 — Parable of unforgiving servant
Genesis 45 — Joseph forgives brothers

Friendly
Luke 6:31
Proverbs 17:17
1 Samuel 18 — David and Jonathan
Acts 9 — Paul and Barnabas

Generosity
Matthew 5:42
Hebrews 13:16
Ruth 2 — Boaz gives grain to Ruth
2 Corinthians 8 — Paul's letter about sharing

Gentle
Matthew 11:29-30
Philippians 4:5
Mark 10 — Jesus and the children
John 19 — Joseph of Arimathea prepares Jesus' body

Genuineness
See sincerity

Giving
See generosity

Goodness
See consistent, holy

Helpfulness
Acts 20:35
Ephesians 6:7-8
Exodus 2 — Miriam and baby Moses
Mark 14 — Disciples prepare Last Supper

Holy
1 Peter 1:15
Psalm 51:10
Acts 10 — Cornelius
Exodus 3 — Moses and the burning bush

Honest
Leviticus 19:11
Ephesians 4:25
Mark 14 — Peter lies about knowing Jesus
1 Samuel 3 — Samuel tells Eli the truth

Honor
See obedient, respectful, reverence

Hopeful
Jeremiah 29:11
Romans 15:13
Acts 1 — Jesus will return/Ascension
Genesis 15 — Abraham looks to the future

Humble
Psalm 25:9
Romans 12:16
Luke 7 — Centurion asks Jesus to heal son
Matthew 3 — John the Baptist and Jesus

Independent
See confident, initiative

Initiative
Joshua 22:5
Ephesians 4:29
John 13 — Jesus washes feet
Nehemiah 2 — Nehemiah asks to go to Jerusalem

Integrity
See consistent, holy, honest

Joyful
1 Thessalonians 5:16
1 Peter 1:8
Luke 2 — Jesus' birth
Acts 12 — Rhoda greets Peter

Justice
See fairness

Kind
1 Thessalonians 5:15
Luke 6:35
2 Samuel 9 — David and Mephibosheth
Acts 28 — Malta islanders and Paul

Knowledge
See teachable

Listening
See attentive

Long-suffering
See patience

Loving
John 13:34-35
1 Corinthians 13:4-7
Luke 15 — Prodigal son
John 11 — Mary, Martha, Lazarus and Jesus

Loyal
1 Chronicles 29:18
Romans 12:5
1 Samuel 20 — David and Jonathan
Ruth 1 — Ruth and Naomi

Meek
See gentle, humble

VALUE BUILDERS SERIES INDEX
BY VALUE

Merciful
Psalm 103:10
Micah 6:8
1 Samuel 25 — Abigail helps David show mercy
Matthew 18 — Unmerciful servant

Obedient
See also respectful
1 Samuel 15:22
Ephesians 6:1
1 Samuel 17 — David takes lunch
Acts 9 — Ananias at Saul's conversion

Patience
Psalm 37: 7
Ephesians 4:2
Genesis 26 — Isaac opens new wells
Nehemiah 6 — Nehemiah stands firm

Peaceful
John 14:27
Hebrews 13:5-6
Acts 12 — Peter sleeping in prison
Matthew 6 — Jesus teaches contentment

Peer pressure, response to
See confident, conviction, wise

Persevering
Galatians 6:9
James 1:2-3
Acts 27 — Paul in shipwreck
Exodus 5 — Moses doesn't give up

Praise
See prayerful, thankful, worshipful

Prayerful
Philippians 4:6
James 5:16
Luke 11 — Jesus teaches disciples
Daniel 6 — Daniel prays daily

Pure
See holy

Purposeful
James 1:22
1 Corinthians 15:58
Matthew 26 — Jesus in Gethsemane
Joshua 24 — Joshua serves God

Reliable
See responsible

Repentant
Acts 26:20
1 John 1:9
Luke 15 — Prodigal son
Luke 22 — Peter's denial

Resourceful
Philippians 4:9
1 Peter 4:10
Luke 5 — Man lowered through roof
Luke 19 — Zacchaeus

Respectful
Deuteronomy 5:16
1 Peter 2:17
1 Samuel 26 — David doesn't kill Saul
Acts 16 — Lydia and other believers

Responsible
Galatians 6:4-5
Proverbs 20:11
Acts 20 — Paul continues his work
Numbers 13 — Caleb follows instructions

Reverence
Daniel 6:26-27
Psalm 78:4, 7
Daniel 3 — Blazing furnace and three Hebrews
Matthew 21 — Triumphal entry

Self-controlled
See self-disciplined

Self-disciplined
1 Timothy 4:7-8
2 Timothy 1:7
Daniel 1 — Daniel and king's meat
John 19 — Jesus was mocked

Self-esteem
See confident

Sensitivity
See empathy, compassionate, concerned, kind

Service (servanthood)
See cooperative, generosity, helpful, stewardship

Sharing
See generosity, stewardship

Sincerity
Romans 12:9
Job 33:3
Mark 5 — Jairus and his daughter
2 Timothy 1 — Timothy

Stewardship
Luke 3:11
Ephesians 5:15-16
2 Chronicles 31 — Temple contributions
Acts 4 — Believers share

Submission
See humble, respectful, self-disciplined

Supportive
See friendly, loving

VALUE BUILDERS SERIES INDEX
BY VALUE

Sympathy
See compassionate, concerned

Teachable
Joshua 1:8
Psalm 32:8
Luke 2 — Young Jesus in the temple
Acts 18 — Apollos with Priscilla and Aquila

Thankful
Psalm 28:17
Colossians 3:17
1 Chronicles 29 — Celebrating the temple
Romans 16 — Paul thanks Phoebe, Priscilla and Aquila

Tolerant
See accepting

Trusting
Proverbs 3:5-6
Psalm 9:10
Acts 27 — Sailors with Paul in shipwreck
2 Kings 18 — Hezekiah trusts God

Trustworthiness
See honest, responsible

Truthful
See honest

Unselfish
Romans 15:1-3
Philippians 2:4
Luke 23 — God gives His Son
John 6 — Boy gives lunch

Wise
Proverbs 8:10
James 3:13
1 Kings 3 — Solomon asks for wisdom
Daniel 1 — Daniel and king's meat

Worshipful
Psalm 86:12
Psalm 122:1
Nehemiah 8 — Ezra and the people worship
Acts 16 — Paul and Silas in jail

VALUE BUILDERS SERIES INDEX
BY SCRIPTURE

Scripture	Story	Value
Genesis 15	Abraham looks to future	Hopeful
Genesis 26	Isaac opens new wells	Patience
Genesis 45	Joseph forgives brothers	Forgiving
Exodus 2	Miriam and baby Moses	Helpful
Exodus 3	Moses and the burning bush	Holy
Exodus 5	Moses doesn't give up	Persevering
Exodus 18	Jethro gives Moses a plan	Cooperative
Leviticus 19:11		Honest
Leviticus 19:15		Fairness
Leviticus 19:18		Forgiving
Numbers 13	Caleb follows instructions	Responsible
Deuteronomy 5:16		Respectful
Deuteronomy 13:6-8		Conviction
Joshua 1:8		Teachable
Joshua 1:9		Courageous
Joshua 22:5		Initiative
Joshua 24	Joshua serves God	Purposeful
Ruth 1	Ruth and Naomi	Loyal
Ruth 2	Boaz gives grain to Ruth	Generosity
1 Samuel 3	Samuel tells Eli the truth	Honest
1 Samuel 15:22		Obedient
1 Samuel 17	David and Goliath	Confident
1 Samuel 17	David takes lunch	Obedient
1 Samuel 18	David and Jonathan	Friendly
1 Samuel 19	Jonathan speaks up for David	Empathy
1 Samuel 20	David and Jonathan	Loyal
1 Samuel 25	Abigail helps David show mercy	Merciful
1 Samuel 26	David doesn't kill Saul	Respectful
2 Samuel 9	David and Mephibosheth	Kind
1 Kings 3	Solomon asks for wisdom	Wise
1 Kings 8:61		Committed
2 Kings 18	Hezekiah trusts God	Trusting
1 Chronicles 29	Celebrating the temple	Thankful
1 Chronicles 29:18		Loyal
2 Chronicles 31	Temple contributions	Stewardship
Nehemiah 2	Nehemiah asks to go to Jerusalem	Initiative
Nehemiah 6	Nehemiah isn't intimidated	Confident
Nehemiah 6	Nehemiah stands firm	Patience
Nehemiah 8	Ezra and the people worship	Worshipful
Nehemiah 8	Ezra reads the law	Attentive
Esther 4	Esther	Committed
Esther 4	Esther	Courageous
Job 33:3		Sincerity
Psalm 9:10		Trusting
Psalm 25:9		Humble
Psalm 28:17		Thankful
Psalm 32:8		Teachable
Psalm 33:4		Consistent
Psalm 34:15		Attentive
Psalm 37:7		Patience
Psalm 51:10		Holy
Psalm 78:4, 7		Reverence
Psalm 86:12		Worshipful
Psalm 103:10		Merciful
Psalm 122:1		Worshipful
Psalm 139:14		Confident
Proverbs 3:5-6		Trusting
Proverbs 8:10		Wise
Proverbs 16:3		Committed
Proverbs 17:17		Friendly
Proverbs 20:11		Responsible
Isaiah 41:10		Courageous
Jeremiah 29:11		Hopeful
Daniel 1	Daniel and king's meat	Self-disciplined
Daniel 1	Daniel and king's meat	Wise
Daniel 3	Blazing furnace and three Hebrews	Conviction
Daniel 3	Blazing furnace and three Hebrews	Reverence
Daniel 6	Daniel as administrator	Consistent
Daniel 6	Daniel prays daily	Prayerful
Daniel 6:26-27		Reverence
Micah 6:8		Merciful
Matthew 3	John the Baptist and Jesus	Humble
Matthew 5:42		Generosity
Matthew 6	Jesus teaches contentment	Peaceful
Matthew 8	Centurion sends servant to Jesus	Faith
Matthew 11:29-30		Gentle
Matthew 18	Unmerciful servant	Merciful
Matthew 18	Parable of unforgiving servant	Forgiving
Matthew 20	Parable of workers	Fairness
Matthew 21	Triumphal entry	Reverence
Matthew 25	Jesus teaches to meet needs	Concerned
Matthew 26	Jesus in Gethsemane	Purposeful
Matthew 26	Jesus in the garden	Consistent
Mark 5	Jairus and his daughter	Sincerity
Mark 10	Jesus and the children	Gentle
Mark 14	Disciples prepare Last Supper	Helpful
Mark 14	Peter lies about knowing Jesus	Honest
Luke 2	Jesus' birth	Joyful
Luke 2	Young Jesus in the temple	Teachable
Luke 3:11		Stewardship
Luke 5	Man lowered through roof	Resourceful
Luke 6:31		Friendly
Luke 6:35		Kind

47

VALUE BUILDERS SERIES INDEX
BY SCRIPTURE

Reference	Topic	Value
Luke 7	Centurion asks Jesus to heal son	Humble
Luke 7	Jesus and woman with no name	Accepting
Luke 10	Good Samaritan	Compassionate
Luke 10	Mary listens to Jesus	Attentive
Luke 11	Jesus teaches disciples	Prayerful
Luke 15	Prodigal son	Loving
Luke 15	Prodigal son	Repentant
Luke 19	Zacchaeus	Resourceful
Luke 22	Peter's denial	Repentant
Luke 23	God gives His Son	Unselfish
Luke 23	Jesus on the cross	Compassionate
John 1	Andrew follows Jesus	Committed
John 2	Jesus clears the temple courts	Conviction
John 3:16		Faith
John 6	Boy gives lunch	Unselfish
John 11	Jesus at Lazarus's death	Empathy
John 11	Mary, Martha, Lazarus, and Jesus	Loving
John 13	Jesus washes feet	Initiative
John 13:34-35		Loving
John 14:27		Peaceful
John 19	Jesus is mocked	Self-disciplined
John 19	Joseph of Arimathea prepares Jesus' body	Gentle
Acts 1	Jesus will return/Ascension	Hopeful
Acts 2	Church provides for each other	Concerned
Acts 4	Believers share	Stewardship
Acts 4:19-20		Conviction
Acts 6	Disciples share responsibilities	Cooperative
Acts 9	Ananias at Saul's conversion	Obedient
Acts 9	Paul and Barnabas	Friendly
Acts 10	Cornelius	Holy
Acts 10	Peter's vision and visit	Accepting
Acts 12	Peter sleeping in prison	Peaceful
Acts 12	Rhoda greets Peter	Joyful
Acts 16	Paul and Silas in jail	Worshipful
Acts 16	Philippian jailer	Faith
Acts 16	Lydia and other believers	Respectful
Acts 18	Apollos with Priscilla and Aquila	Teachable
Acts 20	Paul continues his work	Responsible
Acts 20:35		Helpful
Acts 23	Paul's nephew	Courageous
Acts 26:20		Repentant
Acts 27	Paul in a shipwreck	Persevering
Acts 27	Sailors with Paul in shipwreck	Trusting
Acts 28	Malta islanders with Paul	Kind
Romans 12:5		Loyal
Romans 12:9		Sincerity
Romans 12:16		Humble
Romans 12:17		Fairness
Romans 15:1-3		Unselfish
Romans 15:7		Accepting
Romans 15:13		Hopeful
Romans 16	Paul thanks Phoebe, Priscilla, and Aquila	Thankful
1 Corinthians 12:25		Concerned
1 Corinthians 13:4-7		Loving
1 Corinthians 15:58		Purposeful
2 Corinthians 1:3-4		Compassionate
2 Corinthians 8	Paul's letter about sharing	Generosity
Galatians 3:28		Accepting
Galatians 6:2		Empathy
Galatians 6:4-5		Responsible
Galatians 6:9		Persevering
Ephesians 4:2		Patience
Ephesians 4:16		Cooperative
Ephesians 4:25		Honest
Ephesians 4:29		Initiative
Ephesians 4:32		Forgiving
Ephesians 5:15-16		Stewardship
Ephesians 6:1		Obedient
Ephesians 6:7-8		Helpful
Philippians 2:4		Unselfish
Philippians 4:5		Gentle
Philippians 4:6		Prayerful
Philippians 4:9		Resourceful
Philippians 4:13		Confident
Colossians 3:17		Thankful
Colossians 3:23-24		Cooperative
1 Thessalonians 5:15		Kind
1 Thessalonians 5:16		Joyful
1 Timothy 4:7-8		Self-disciplined
2 Timothy 1	Timothy	Sincerity
2 Timothy 1:7		Self-disciplined
Hebrews 11:6		Faith
Hebrews 13:3		Empathy
Hebrews 13:5-6		Peaceful
Hebrews 13:16		Generosity
James 1:2-3		Persevering
James 1:19		Attentive
James 1:22		Purposeful
James 2	Favoritism at a meeting	Fairness
James 3:13		Wise
James 5:16		Prayerful
1 Peter 1:8		Joyful
1 Peter 1:15		Holy
1 Peter 2:17		Respectful
1 Peter 3:8		Compassionate
1 Peter 4:10		Resourceful
1 John 1:9		Repentant
1 John 3:17		Concerned
1 John 3:18		Consistent